PORTFOLIO E

METROPOLITAN SEMINARS IN ART

Great Periods in Painting

PORTFOLIO E

The World In Order: THE HIGH RENAISSANCE

BY JOHN CANADAY

ART EDITOR AND CRITIC
THE NEW YORK TIMES

THE METROPOLITAN MUSEUM OF ART

THE WORLD IN ORDER

The High Renaissance

OUR TWO preceding discussions followed the Italian Renaissance as it developed during the wonderfully inventive fifteenth century, first in Florence and then in the rest of Italy. While northern European artists were continuing the mystical tradition of the Middle Ages, the Italians were rediscovering the world around them, investigating it as scientists, and finding a new relationship with classical antiquity. Their new joy in life and their fervent curiosity about the nature of the world led them to an understanding of the pagan Greeks and Romans; they studied ancient philosophers and poets with new sympathy, revived their traditions, emulated them, brought the Olympian gods back from exile, and by the end of the century had come close to the perfect harmony and order that was the classical ideal in art and thought.

The sixteenth century saw the culmination of the classical ideal in the High Renaissance in Italy. It also saw the end of the medieval tradition in the north, when renaissance art, transplanted to the soil of France, took root and flourished there. In addition, it saw a re-

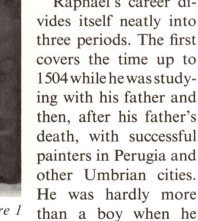

Figure 1

volt against the classical ideal. These critical developments are the subject of this portfolio.

Raphael

The career of Raffaello Sanzio, called Raphael, is the great success story of the Renaissance. He was born in 1483 when the early Renaissance was reaching its zenith. By the time he died in 1520, at the age of only thirty-seven, he had brought renaissance science and renaissance classicism into full harmony. Born the son of an obscure provincial painter, Raphael died the intimate friend of popes and princes. The ingredients of his success were great talent, charm, intelligence, and industry.

Raphael's career divides itself neatly into three periods. The first covers the time up to 1504 while he was studying with his father and then, after his father's death, with successful painters in Perugia and other Umbrian cities. He was hardly more than a boy when he painted the two charming minor lyrics we have seen, *The Vision of a Knight* (Plate C7) and *The Three Graces* (Plate D12). As a youth he re-

Figure 2

ceived good commissions for altarpieces; he painted religious pictures of great sweetness in the manner of Perugino, with whom he probably studied and acted as assistant.

But Umbria offered Raphael something less than full scope for the development of his potential as a major artist. In 1504, at the age of twenty-one, he went to Florence, where he stayed for four years. These years were not spectacularly successful from the point of view of major commissions, but the young man found plenty of work doing various religious pictures and portraits. Florence gave him an opportunity to study the art of its great men, and Raphael began transforming his gentle lyricism into the grandeur that was to be demanded by his century. *Madonna and Child Enthroned with Saints* (*Figure 1*), painted at the dividing point between his Umbrian and his Florentine periods, shows that already Raphael was beginning to discipline his forms

in the direction of greater monumentality.

In Florence Raphael studied the art of Donatello, who was a potent influence for more than a generation after his death, a kind of demigod for artists; of Pollaiuolo, who had died while Raphael was still a student; and of a young man called Michelangelo who was only eight years older than Raphael but already a leading artist. All these men were creative spirits of a force and a vitality far removed from Raphael's sweetly poetic style. Taking them as his models strengthened and enlarged Raphael's forms and saved him from the danger of exhausting a limited manner, one that in Perugino became so repetitious and cloying.

Raphael particularly admired another artist, in his middle fifties, who had painted a Last Supper (Portfolio 6, Plate 61) in Milan about a decade before and had recently completed the portrait *Mona Lisa* (Portfolio 1, Plate 6). Leonardo da Vinci's grace and his apparent

6

Figure 3

serenity tempered the more robust grandeur inspired by the other artists Raphael admired. A synthesis of serenity and grandeur was to become Raphael's hallmark. The searching, questioning nature of Leonardo's intellect and the inner restlessness that found expression in the curious smile of *Mona Lisa* escaped Raphael. What he absorbed in Florence completed his education for his Roman assignments, fitting him for his role as the artist who gave final expression to the renaissance conviction that through the intellectualization of experience man could discover in life a perfect harmony and order.

The nature of Raphael's synthesis should be made apparent by a comparison of his *Alba Madonna* (Plate E1), painted in Rome after he had assimilated the lessons of both Umbria and Florence, with a Florentine masterpiece of the last years of the century, Filippino Lippi's *Holy Family with Saint Margaret and Saint John* (Plate E2), both circular compositions.

Filippino Lippi (about 1457–1504) was the natural son of that unregenerate Fra Filippo Lippi, whose work we have seen, and Lucrezia Buti. Trained by his father and by Botticelli, Filippino was a popular artist whose commissions included completing Masaccio's murals in the Brancacci Chapel, left unfinished upon that great painter's death. Filippino was a good Florentine, reflecting the various influences current in the second half of his century. In *The Holy Family* we see the familiar devices—the bit of renaissance architecture, the inventive landscape, the detailed complications of drapery, the realism in the representation of Saint Joseph, the triangular composition (modified here to meet the demands of the circular shape), plus the rather special influence of Botticelli. The color, bright and pure, has the clear tonalities of tempera. This clarity is matched by the grace of the figures

7

and the flow of line along hands, arms, veils, and robes, uniting the figures in rhythmic patterns across the panel's surface. It is a charming picture, full of interest from passage to passage and even suggesting, in the rather unexpected massiveness of the figure of the Madonna, an effort toward monumentality as well as tenderness.

This quality, monumentality, is the dominant one in Raphael's *Alba Madonna*. Beside Raphael's composition, Filippino's seems prolix. Raphael's forms are simplified into broad

Alinari   *Figure 4*

masses; they build upon and support one another with the solidity of architecture; except for the logic and harmony of their proportions they might even seem ponderous. The effect, for this reason, is one of greater dignity than that of *The Holy Family*, but since the inner spiritual sweetness remains, *The Alba Madonna*

is a similar statement that suggests deeper significance. This impression is increased by the greater breadth of the landscape, which makes Filippino's seem cluttered. In every part Raphael conceives his picture as a structure of three-dimensional volumes in three-dimensional space; Filippino's remains essentially flat. The earlier composition ornaments a circular area, a disk; Raphael's occupies a globular volume. It is imperative, if we are to receive the full effect of *The Alba Madonna*, to regard the painted forms not as a flow of line into line but as a structure of masses within this sphere. On the other hand, if we look at Filippino's composition in this way it falls to pieces and loses the balance and rhythm that unite it as a flat design.

Both methods of composing have their special advantages, of course, but Raphael's way allows for fuller harmonies, wider rhythms, more profound serenities. As long ago as the first of our discussions we saw a portrait by Renoir (Portfolio 1, Plate 3) in which the figure was reduced to solid oval and cylindrical forms building upon one another. We pointed out that the fundamental nature of a symbol is somehow best expressed through simple geometrical forms. Although Renoir was painting a woman as a symbol of earth and fertility and Raphael was painting a symbol of another nature, both painters give their symbols impressive dignity by organizing them as geometrical solids in compact harmony. The resemblance is not coincidental, for Renoir painted his portrait after he had made a trip to Rome expressly to study Raphael. His goal on this pilgrimage was the series of frescoes Raphael painted in the papal apartments of the Vatican. (Renoir would equally have admired *The Alba Madonna*, but it was out of reach in the Russian imperial collection.)

These Vatican frescoes, Raphael's summation of renaissance ideals, occupied him from 1509 until he died. Many of them were executed by his pupils and followers after his death; some had been executed largely by

8

Figure 5

Figure 6

these assistants even during Raphael's life-time, for he had surrounded himself with helpers as he became flooded with commissions. His great patrons were Popes Julius II and Leo X, both of whom were determined to make Rome outshine the grandeur of its ancient days. Raphael also served the popes as architect, interior designer, and director of antiquities. He was virtually a prince of Rome, moving about the city with an elegant retinue.

Before we consider the Vatican frescoes we might look at Raphael's *Count Tommaso Inghirami* (Plate E3), portraying one of the circle of powerful and brilliant men who were his intimates and patrons.

Tommaso Inghirami (1470–1516) was a canon of Saint Peter's, poet laureate to Emperor Maximilian (with the privilege of adding the Austrian eagle to his coat of arms), a Palatine count, Librarian of the Vatican, Secretary to the Fifth Lateran Council and to

the College of Cardinals, the most fashionable preacher in Rome, and a scholar of such eminence that both Erasmus and Ariosto boasted of his friendship. As a churchman he wholeheartedly admired the antique cultivation in which fluent scholarship was more important than religious conviction, social and political aplomb far more important than any concern with spiritual values. He captivated everyone he met by his wit, his festive manner, and his piercing intelligence. Once when the performance of a play by Seneca was interrupted, he took over and entertained the audience by improvising Roman verse in the classical manner. Such a man typified Raphael's Rome. A similar group that had surrounded Lorenzo de' Medici in Florence seems quiet and intimate by comparison. Inghirami was in fact Lorenzo's protégé: when Inghirami's father was killed by the Florentines in the sack of Volterra, where the family

10

belonged to the nobility, the two-year-old boy was taken by Lorenzo and raised under his protection until, at thirteen, he was sent to Rome to begin his career in the Church.

Raphael's portrait of this man is as incisive as the man himself. He is shown in the scarlet cloth of his post as Secretary to the Lateran Council, alert as he waits at the moment of taking notes. Inghirami had a conspicuous cast in his right eye. His upward glance accounts for much of the impression of keen attention that makes the portrait so exceptional, but it also serves to minimize this defect without recourse to an extraneous device.

The Vatican Frescoes

The Vatican frescoes, then, were conceived against the intellectual background of men like Tommaso Inghirami and the papal determination to increase and celebrate the majesty of classical Rome. We will look at two of the frescoes, *The School of Athens* and *The Disputation on the Eucharist*, both in the same apartment and both from Raphael's own hand, except for the routine passages always left to assistants in works as large as these. They are, unfortunately, the kind of pictures that should be seen at full scale in their own

Figure 7

Anderson

Figure 8

setting; here we must see them enormously reduced, to the size of a page in a book. But even so, we may see that the philosophers in *The School of Athens* (*Figure 2*) move or stand majestically within grand space, space defined by one of those painted renaissance buildings that are among the architectural masterpieces of the time.

In *The Disputation* (*Figure 3*) the clouds that, on a page, seem to be a band running across a flat wall should be read instead as an arc making its half-circle back into space, echoing the real arch that frames the fresco. The two curved forms might almost be hinged together, with the painted one at a 90° angle behind the actual one. The saints sit in a formal row around the enthroned Christ, with God the Father above and the dove of the Holy Spirit below. In the earthly part of the picture the half-circle into depth is subtly repeated. The arrangement reaches its focus and the theme its climax at an altar bearing the wafer that, in the service of the Mass, is the body of Christ. The two halves of the composition, upper and lower, are united by the strictly vertical relationship of the monstrance holding the wafer and the relationship of its circle, the larger circle enclosing the dove, and the still larger one framing the nimbus around Christ. The subject, a theological discussion of

the portion of the Mass in which the wafer figures, is not a "dispute" but a picturization of theological dogma. *The School of Athens*, with Plato and Aristotle at its center, contrasts the idea of free discussion with this idea of dogma.

In both compositions Raphael is less an innovator than a supremely skillful and sophisticated eclectic designer who applies principles worked out by his predecessors. *The School of Athens*, though it is more subtle and more complicated, continues to use Perugino's compositional devices, while the strict geometrical skeleton of *The Disputation* owes a great deal to Leonardo's *Last Supper*. Raphael's greatness lies not in his powers of invention but in the harmony and control with which he fuses the contributions of more emphatically individual artists. He unified into a single statement the multiple statements of men who were great in different ways. As a result, he is less exciting than the men who created the material with which he works, less stimulating than the innovators of the preceding century. Yet he is their summation. We must accept the fact that their various contributions, fused, necessarily temper one another; they lose intensity in reaching harmony.

For some people "nullify" would be more apt than "temper." For them Raphael's frescoes are gigantic bores, though few are heretical enough to admit it. But Raphael's detractors are likely to admit that even if he is only the competent synthesizer of other men's discoveries, he is the one artist who demonstrates that competence may approach genius. And for most people and most artists over the centuries since Raphael, the Vatican frescoes do achieve at last that intellectual order that renaissance thinkers hoped to synthesize from the chaotic material of human experience.

Venice

Venice, a unique world, is always special, lying beyond the generalities that apply to

Figure 9

other places, and as would be expected, her painters created their own special version of a world in order.

Raphael's harmonies are intellectual; those of the Venetians are sensuous. The painter Giorgione (about 1478–1510), who was born five years before Raphael, lived an even shorter life, dying when he was about thirty-two just as Raphael was starting the first of the Vatican frescoes. But in those few years he set the direction for Venetian painting of the High Renaissance.

We have already seen *The Tempest* (Portfolio 12, Plate 133), one of four paintings (out of a total of sixteen attributed to Giorgione) that are unquestionably by him. Another picture, *The Concert* (Plate E4), belongs to a second group that most scholars are willing to accept as Giorgione's; the rest are more dubious and the subject of endless and futile debate.

If *The Concert* is not by Giorgione, it is the work of an extraordinarily fine painter influenced by him. Giorgione's impact was tremendous; it not only determined the character of sixteenth-century Venetian art but it affected painters throughout Europe during his time and has done so recurrently ever since.

"The Concert" is a moderately appropriate designation, not Giorgione's, given to a picture whose title has been lost, if it ever had one, and which hardly seems to need one. If the problematical first meanings of the picture are eventually rediscovered, as they have been for Piero di Cosimo's Vulcan cycle, perhaps *The Concert* will be enlarged and enriched for us as Piero's pictures were. But one would be almost reluctant to discover here some didactic symbolism, or some story, behind an inexplicable combination of opulent nudes, grassy banks, lush foliage, gleaming satins, and golden light, or to discover why one of the nudes pours water from a crystal pitcher into a well.

The picture is more than a visual harmony; it appeals to the sense of touch as well, making us aware of the feel of herbage, fabrics, and flesh, of the warmth of sun and the coolness of shade. We can imagine the sound of the silvery trickle of water and the vibrant notes of plucked strings. These harmonies of the senses are presented in a composition that seems as casual as Raphael's is disciplined, yet the picture is as orderly and as balanced in its way as *The School of Athens* or *The Disputation*.

Giorgione probably studied with Giovanni Bellini, whose *Feast of the Gods* (Plate D11) was completed in Bellini's very old age after the death of Giorgione. The student may have influenced the master here, for *The Feast of the Gods* has much of Giorgione's poetic quality. But Bellini had been developing in the same direction, as his earlier *Madonna Enthroned with Four Saints* (*Figure 4*) shows, its formal arrangement poeticized by luminosity and moody suggestion, to which his students in Giorgione's generation were to add the typical Venetian sumptuousness.

According to the early art historian Vasari,

Figure 10

14

Figure 11

The Feast of the Gods was completed by a young painter (who probably knew Giorgione in Bellini's workshop), Tiziano Vecellio, called Titian (1477/87–1576), who became the greatest Venetian painter of them all.

As Giorgione's immediate influence faded, Titian's color became bolder, his compositions more tempestuous, his religious themes more emotionalized, his pagan subjects more voluptuous. But in spite of these qualities Titian's art continued the transmutation of the stuff of sensuous experience into poetry. It gloried in the good things of this world and celebrated its physical delights, elevating them beyond the triviality and transience of everyday life. Titian's *Rape of Europa* (Plate E5) is

an exultant picture. The lordly bull bears away his prize through a world pulsating with light, through radiant air and shining water, where perfection is not a matter of ultimate serenities or exquisite refinements but of the full realization of the delight of the senses.

This is Titian's expression of the ideal of fullness and completeness sought by the High Renaissance. He pushes everything—rich color, luscious form, a painted surface that in itself is a sensuous delight—just to the point of exaggeration or excess but not beyond. In its way this balance is as complete as Raphael's. Titian holds to the classical renaissance ideal of control, as opposed to romantic abandon, even in pictures like *The Rape of Europa* where he seems on the verge of violating it. The picture remains self-contained: it is a brimming cup but it does not spill over.

It can be compared, to the disadvantage of neither, with Francesco di Giorgio's version of the subject (Plate D9), an example of early renaissance classicism modified by the sweet nostalgia of late Sienese painting. And in another direction a comparison between Titian's version and that of another Venetian, Veronese (Paolo Caliari, 1528–1588), may be equally enlightening.

A native of Verona, as his nickname indicates, Veronese became a favorite decorator of palaces and public buildings as Venice continued to build and paint itself into the most luxuriantly decorated city in the world. His *Triumph of Venice* (*Figure 5*), the central panel from the ceiling of the Great Council Chamber in the Doges' Palace, is typical of the elaborately staged pageants that Veronese painted again and again in a purely secular spirit. Even

Figure 12

when he was representing religious subjects like *The Wedding Feast at Cana* (*Figure 6*) Veronese ignored the nominal subject to paint instead a Venetian feast attended by the richly costumed dignitaries of a city still flowing with gold from her commerce with the East.

His *Rape of Europa* (Plate E6) has the air of an incident from princely social life. The subject could not very well be translated directly into a contemporary banquet hall or ballroom scene, yet Europa and her attendants are quite obviously a Venetian lady of high station and her retinue of gentlewomen. Even the bull behaves with the social decorum of a great noble. The abduction is staged with all the elegant display of a reception for a visiting potentate. It is a magnificent picture, for Veronese was a magnificent painter, but when we compare it with Titian's version or with Giorgione's *The Concert*, we see that the rich stuffs, the finely fleshed human beings, and the luxuriant foliage have lost their lyrical quality and have become a celebration of wealth, display, and physical beauty for their own sakes. Veronese's grandeur, in short, is more mundane than poetic. The poetry that was so gentle in Giorgione and so richly full-blown in Titian begins to coarsen into a more obvious and worldly interest in physical opulence. In Veronese we have the first hint of a decline, the first suggestion that the Venetian world could no longer sustain an art of great expressive depth.

But while Veronese was staging his pageants, Titian, by this time an old man, was painting with increased power. After they reach middle age, artists of small soul or merely facile talent are likely to deny their youthful promise by resorting to sterile repetitions or variations on their early successes, becoming parasites upon their former selves, like second-rate followers. But great ones paint to the end with deepening power, growing upon themselves, nourished by their early work to achieve finally a consummate expression of their promise. Titian, who lived to the age of ninety or perhaps to the

Archives Photographiques, Paris

Figure 13

edge of a hundred (his birth date is uncertain), was such a painter. His *Pietà* (*Figure 7*) is one of the most moving of all Christian pictures, phenomenal in having been produced in a materialistic society by an artist whose work had included pictures as ebulliently pagan as *The Rape of Europa*. The golden light that shot through Europa's glorious world now glows more somberly upon the dead Christ (*Figure 8*); the full forms and ample gestures that were so triumphant are now majestic expressions of the tragedy and joy of a miracle of the spirit.

Titian began the picture in 1573, to hang over his own tomb. After his death in 1576 final touches were added by a pupil but they are negligible in the total effect. Technically the painting is the climax of a lifelong development in which lines and edges tended to disappear as forms were built up more and more by pigment applied in broken strokes in the areas of light and thin films in the shadows (*Figure 9*). It is possible that the failing sight and the waning physical energy of a very old man played a part in the exaggeration of this technique toward the end, but the spiritual vigor, the strength of conception, and above all the discipline of a lifetime of study are apparent in each stroke of the brush. These strokes are juxtaposed rather than pulled together, a technical device that increases the vibrancy of the painting of light; three hundred years later it was adopted by the impressionists as the technical basis of their art.

The Mannerists

In the meantime, first in Florence and then in Rome and still later in northern Italy, a group of painters revolted against Raphael's clas-

17

Alinari

Figure 14

sicism. *The School of Athens* and *The Disputation*, we have said, represented the perfect order for which the Renaissance had yearned, whose existence in the universal scheme of things it had never doubted. But the impersonality of this Raphaelesque order held the seed of monotony. And even more important, the times no longer supported the orderly assumptions of classical thought. Military defeats, financial crises, and the increasingly flagrant corruption of the Church created an uneasiness that was reflected in art, either by the artist's retreat into himself or by his rejection of classical statement for another that expressed the restless and ominous atmosphere around him. The latter expression found itself in the late paintings of Michelangelo.

The former, a retreat into estheticism, was the choice of the mannerist painters, who now set about the cultivation of extremely individual styles in a search for variety and a means to express intense feelings in more personal ways than were offered by the serene and generalized forms of Raphael's classical model. When this effort failed their work is merely bizarre, depending on distortions that may seem meaningless to the observer who does not share the painter's special response.

Hence mannerism has been until recently a derogatory term, indicating a self-conscious school of painting, the cultivation of individuality at any cost, a shallow, fashionable eccentricity. But mannerism is now an honest word, joining others (for instance, "gothic" and "impressionist") that were also derogatory at one time. The expressive intensity of mannerist painting has been revealed, unexpectedly enough, by the art of modern painters like Van Gogh, Gauguin, and other postimpressionists who had to find similarly highly personal styles as expressions of their similar efforts to find some kind of meaning in a chaotic world.

For the record we set down the names of Pontormo, Rosso, and Parmigianino as conspicuous leaders in the mannerist revolt, but we will illustrate the work of only one painter,

Figure 15

Bronzino (1503–1572), a member of the second mannerist generation in Florence.

Bronzino developed a precise, rigid style that was most effective in works like *Portrait of a Young Man* (Plate E7). His sharp edges, his enamel-like surface, and his way of holding his color unrelentingly within clearly defined areas might lead us to mistake him for a painter of the early Renaissance. But Bronzino was painting at a time when free technique, a richer surface, and considerable flexibility in color had been made possible by the replacement of tempera by oil. Therefore, Bronzino's somewhat atavistic use of line and color is close to affectation, no matter how effective it may be—and it is effective in the extreme. The term "mannerist" is unusually descriptive; it connotes a deliberately calculated style cultivated at the expense of expressive depth. Bronzino's beautiful portraits lack interpretative variety. Everyone he paints takes on practically the same haughty air of wealth and consequence.

By one interpretation Bronzino is nothing

Figure 17

more than a smart stylist. Nothing much seems to go on beneath the slightly tinny surfaces of his beautifully designed faces; his rigidly applied formula reduces his subjects to attractive manikins.

But by another interpretation his subjects are not manikins but individuals who keep themselves to themselves. Their impassive and unyielding faces are masks behind which the individual lives in his own world of private speculations. This extreme reserve was reflected in certain of the ducal courts of the time, where the most rigid etiquette replaced the intellectual bonhomie of the early renaissance gatherings of, for instance, Lorenzo de' Medici.

In subject pictures also the mannerists were more interested in pure esthetics than in direct expression. Here again Bronzino offers an example. His *Allegory* (*Figure 10*) is a meticulously involuted exercise based on a swastika pattern. It is an exceedingly decorative panel but no amount of trying can convince us that it has much interest as an allegory. The picture's expressive content must be found in-

Figure 16

19

directly: the complicated interweavings of its composition reflect intense absorption in limited problems examined at close range, a way of thought that had replaced the classical one of universal breadth. The shifting balances and active pattern reflect the restlessness of an age no longer convinced that the chaos of the world could be intellectualized into a universal harmony, an age forced to discover satisfactions in small complications rather than grand simplicities.

Except for its beguiling erotic contrivances, *An Allegory* is art for art's sake, design for the sake of design, technique for the sake of technique. For this reason Bronzino is more interesting to painters today than he has been for a long time. The purely esthetic approach of much modern abstract painting is more sympathetic to Bronzino's preoccupation with style and theory than is the opposite attitude, which demands that a picture "say something"

Figure 19

or appeal to our emotions through images that we can relate to nonintellectual experience.

North of the Alps

We have seen that while the Renaissance was developing and reaching its climax in Italy, northern artists continued in the medieval tradition. Grünewald painted the incomparable Isenheim altarpiece (*Figure 23*, Plates B11 and B12) several years after Raphael had completed the Vatican frescoes.

But now, in France, a fashionable and intellectual revolution took place under a king whose personality dominated his time to an unprecedented extent. Francis I (1494–1547), "the long-nosed king with night life in his eye," started a practice that would eventually grow into a national policy of patronage of the arts. The building and decoration of palaces that stood as symbols of the power of the king (as well as appropriate settings for high living) continued until the French Revolution.

Francis wanted his court artists to catch up overnight with Italy's attainments in painting, sculpture, and architecture. He set about closing the hundred-year gap by importing

Figure 18

Figure 20

gious, quasi-amorous allegories. *The Birth of Cupid* (*Figure 11*), a typical example of the Fontainebleau style, would have been inconceivable even by the most relaxed standards of late medieval art. The painting was formerly attributed to Francesco Primaticcio (1504–1570), the Italian mannerist who left the strongest mark on French art, but it is now given to one of the many anonymous followers who worked with him and very much in his style. Primaticcio organized much of the decorative scheme of the palace at Fontainebleau, continued as major-domo for Francis' son, Henry II, and finally went to Paris as chief decorator for Henry's wife, Catherine de' Medici. He created the type of the standard Fontainebleau nude, seen in the recumbent Venus of *The Birth of Cupid*, long-limbed, with tiny head, hands, and feet, full thighs and hips, small high breasts, and silken blond hair.

Italian artists to make his palace at Fontainebleau a monument to the new culture.

But skipping a hundred of the most crowded years in the development of painting and transplanting the end result in full flower from its natural habitat to foreign soil and climate was bound to result in artificialities, especially since Francis and his court were interested in the grace and elegance of renaissance art rather than its philosophical basis. Francis imported great artists like Leonardo da Vinci and Andrea del Sarto, but the ones most active in the creation of the "school of Fontainebleau" were more superficial. The resultant style took on something of the look of an exotic plant in a greenhouse. The school was made up of imported Italian artists and their French and Flemish followers, who, abandoning all vestiges of medievalism, adopted an Italianate worldliness and affectation.

We have already seen, in discussing the Unicorn tapestries (Portfolio B, *Figure 22*), that this worldliness and courtly sensitivity had made its appearance in French art as the age of faith waned. But now at Fontainebleau it came without disguise. Naked goddesses replaced heavily robed chatelaines, and the open celebration of love replaced quasi-reli-

Figure 21

The type received its most beautiful summary in *Diana* (Plate E8) by an anonymous French painter. Diana (the Greek Artemis) was the goddess of the moon and the hunt; of all goddesses she is the one dedicated to the most invulnerable chastity. But the Dianas that appear again and again in French art of this period are not Dianas at all, but Venuses. They are tributes to a lady who bore Diana's name but not her character—Diane de Poitiers, who as Henry II's mistress was the reigning goddess of love—and, secondarily, tributes to the goddess of the hunt, although the popularity of this sport reached the level of a court function.

Diane is also commemorated in sculpture in the exquisite *Diana and the Stag* (*Figure 12*) by Jean Goujon (1510?–1566?), the first great classicist in French art. He modified the excessive mannerisms of the school of Fontainebleau by more direct classical reference and a sensitivity to the spirit of ancient Greece that would have been exceptional even in one of those Italians who first responded to antiquity. In his *Diana*, Venus and all that she stood for in the arts and in life completed the journey that began when she was wafted to the shores of Italy in Botticelli's picture (Plate D1). She fell in love with France, and, like so many other people since then, she has remained there as a happy expatriate.

Goujon's *Diana and the Stag* was carved for

Anderson

Figure 22

22

the château of Anet, Henry II's gift to Diane de Poitiers and one of the string of châteaux that now grew up near Paris and along the Loire river. Ranging in magnificence from palaces to intimate country houses, they found their ancestors in medieval fortified castles. With the addition of Italianate classical elements, they became lovely hybrids. The guard towers and donjons became decorative fantasies; the moats, originally protection against besiegers, became ornamental bodies of water reflecting pinnacles, turrets, fanciful moldings, and delicious carving (*Figure 13*). The military fortress had become a stronghold of pleasure and the arts.

The look of the aristocrats who inhabited the châteaux has been preserved for us in a large group of portraits and portrait drawings by Jean Clouet (active by 1516–died 1540) and his son François, who succeeded his father as court painter to Francis I and then to Henry II, Francis II, and Charles IX. Jean Clouet was not much affected by Italianisms, which were imported when he was already a mature artist; his portrait of Francis I (*Figure 14*) is still close to the native tradition of direct, objective portraiture as it had crystallized in the last part of the fifteenth century.

François Clouet (active by 1536–died 1572) also painted portraits in this tradition, like *Guy XVII, Count of Laval* (Plate E9), but he often adopted elements from the "modern" style of Fontainebleau, usually with the lessening of vigor that might be expected. Sometimes a work of his fell altogether within the school, like the portrait of a fine lady in her bathtub (*Figure 15*), one of a series of such pictures by Clouet and other artists that were sometimes unblushingly erotic. The model for Clouet's relatively restrained treatment of the curious theme was probably Diane de Poitiers herself.

The Clouets have left us as great a legacy in their small portrait drawings as in their more formal paintings. Usually executed in pink and black tones on lightly tinted paper, they are a roster of the inhabitants of the châteaux, who

Anderson

Figure 23

exchanged these informal portraits with one another as souvenirs of an occasion or as tokens of friendship. (Accounts of life along the Loire during the season when the aristocrats moved down from Paris make it sound like a succession of house parties devoted to hunting and dancing.) Both father and son were expert draughtsmen; their drawings (*Figure 16*) are executed with a directness and delicacy that often make their paintings seem labored by comparison. As so many drawings do, these bring us closer to the artist than more elaborate work does; we are closer to the sitters also, who for the space of an hour or so posed informally and have continued ever since to look at us with the interested expressions of people who are intensely curious to see how their pictures are going to turn out.

The Reformation

While Francis's court was the center of this fashionable revolution, Germany was the center of a religious, social, and economic one—the Reformation. When the great reformer Martin Luther visited Rome in 1510–1511 (while Raphael was working on the Vatican frescoes) he observed the lax religious conditions there—a continuation of those against which Savonarola had preached more than a dozen years before. When Luther publicly condemned certain practices of the Church, he was excommunicated.

The Germany that produced a Luther and accepted his reforms was likely to express itself in different terms than the Italy that had produced a Savonarola but rejected him or a France that adopted Venus with enthusiasm. These terms were practical rather than artistic, the country's energy apparently having been spent in housecleaning and reorganization. It takes some difficult critical gymnastics to establish a close connection between the Reformation and the arts. Some writers see the Isenheim altarpiece as a prophetic expression of the Reformation, pointing out that the adherents of the movement did not regard

Alinari

Figure 24

Figure 25

dispose a few simple elements to concentrate interest on a face. He paints its features with such an appearance of objectivity that we are likely to miss the subtle emphases that transform it from a literal image into the projection of a personality.

In his drawings, usually studies for portraits painted without the model, he not only sets down the bulk and disposition of the sitter's features in a few lines and a touch or two of shading but records the nature of the person (*Figure 18*). Holbein was not interested in beautifying his subjects. Nor was he a formula painter. Each portrait is a new problem for him—he makes adjustments in the head, the disposition of the body, and the patterning of details of the costume in order to individualize a person. We analyzed a particularly subtle example in *Christina of Denmark* (Portfolio 5, Plate 55).

Lucas Cranach (1472–1553), who was twenty-five years older than Holbein, is an artist of an entirely different character. He stands alone in the Germany of his time as a painter of delightful sophistications. Although he was a fervent admirer and close friend of Luther, whose portrait (*Figure 19*) and that of his wife (*Figure 20*) he painted, and a loyal adherent of the Reformation, his most individual works were pagan subjects interpreted with sly, tongue-in-cheek wittiness. He does not take *The Judgment of Paris* (Plate E11) very seriously; he half satirizes the mannerists and, in a way, surpasses them at their own game of eccentric style and impeccable technique. His slant-eyed, pert-nosed, delicate-boned little goddesses also appear as bourgeois minxes and court ladies. They even appear as the heroines of Bible stories, assuming an appropriate gravity in roles for which they are not perfectly cast. The woman in *Judith with the Head of Holofernes* (*Figure 21*), whose arm rests with such style upon the head that she has just severed, is more interested in her elaborate toilette than in her supposedly gory and self-sacrificial experience.

themselves as rebels against Catholicism but only as reformers of the parent church, stimulating a rebirth of mystical expression as opposed to the humanism of Italian religious painting of the time. And Dürer's *Melancolia I* (Portfolio 10, *Figure 9*), with its agony of doubt, is sometimes interpreted as a response to the disturbed times. Other writers feel that the Reformation was fatal to art and responsible for the relatively small production of painting in Germany in the sixteenth century.

Whatever the reason, it is true that after the death in 1528 of both Grünewald and Dürer, themselves so different from one another, Germany offers occasional individual painters rather than a school of painters united by anything like a common style. Two of these artists, Hans Holbein the Younger (1497–1543) and Lucas Cranach the Elder, are often called mannerists, the first with little justification, the second with much.

After a successful career in Germany and Switzerland Holbein went to England in 1526 and in 1536 became court painter to Henry VIII. His elaborate portrait of Henry (*Figure 17*), which lies at one end of Holbein's scale, may be a little oppressive in the overpowering richness of its detail. At the other end, his *Member of the Wedigh Family* (Plate E10) demonstrates the certainty with which he could

Michelangelo

We have seen, then, the climax of the classical aspirations of the Renaissance in Raphael, a comparable climax in the Venetian world of Titian, followed by the rejection of the classical ideal by the mannerists in Italy and their followers, or analogous painters, in northern Europe. But in tracing this story we have bypassed the titanic Michelangelo with no more than a reference to the fact that the young Raphael, in Florence, studied the art of this slightly older contemporary.

Michelangelo Buonarroti (1475–1564) has been left until the conclusion of this discussion because his art is a bridge to the next century. He, in his own way, also summarized the renaissance ideal, but in an even more important way he denied it. His denial was not in the nature of a retreat into estheticism like that of

mannerists of Bronzino's type but a progression of gigantic achievements that treated the human spirit in terms of the new age.

While Raphael was painting the Vatican frescoes, Michelangelo was working on the frescoes of the Sistine Ceiling, just a short walk away. Michelangelo was a homely, difficult, tormented, quarrelsome, and even solitary man. Like Raphael, he was courted by popes, but he did the Sistine Ceiling under protest and once fled the pope's service and had to be brought back under what amounted to arrest.

Raphael was always conscious of Michelangelo's vital presence nearby and aware, it seems, of the greater power of Michelangelo's work, for Raphael's last pictures show the influence of the more dramatic grandeur, the sweep and rush and restlessness of Michelangelo's art. Raphael, the perfect courtier, failed to assimilate this power; in his history

Alinari

Figure 26

26

Alinari
Figure 27

of intelligent eclecticism, this was Raphael's only defeat.

Michelangelo's Sistine Ceiling tells the story of the creation of the world and man, of man's temptation and fall, then of his second chance when the evil of the world was wiped out by the Flood. The good man Noah and his family were saved, but the story ends with man's second fall, through Noah's drunkenness after the Flood. Thus, although the figures in Michelangelo's drama have the superhuman stature of gods (*Figure 22*), they remain men in their frailty. The theme is not that of a world intellectualized into perfect order but that of a world that can never be so ordered because man himself is imperfect.

But this tragic premise is raised from pessimism to a prediction of joy by the rows of prophets (*Figure 23*) who by foretelling the coming of Christ promise man redemption in spite of his weakness. Thus the Sistine Ceiling plays two themes in counterpoint—man's

tragic frailty and God's infinite compassion. We can argue that in creating this balance of forces Michelangelo gave expression to the renaissance ideal of perfect order, but this great work is such a stupendous conception that anyone who studies it finds various meanings in it.

One thing is certain: in the three decades that separate the Sistine Ceiling from the later work in the same chapel, *The Last Judgment* on the end wall, the pessimistic elements in Michelangelo's art increased in response to personal difficulties and to the troubles of the times, foreign invasions at home and the spread of the Reformation abroad, that affected the mannerists. The mannerists in fact fed generously upon Michelangelo when they rejected Raphael; they adopted Michelangelesque forms but never approached the grandeur of conception that these forms served.

As an instance, the Medici tombs, which Michelangelo executed between 1524 and 1534, after the Sistine Ceiling and before *The Last Judgment*, are by any standard superbly decorative. As examples of pure style, the four figures of Night, Day, Morning, and Evening are stunning. But Michelangelo's figures are great works of expressive sculpture. In them the elements of confidence and hope that modify the pessimism of the Sistine Ceiling have largely disappeared. The figure symbolizing Morning awakes in weariness and pain; Evening sinks into melancholy brooding; Day is restless, disturbed (*Figures 24* and *25*); Night sleeps fitfully (*Figure 26*). Their comfortless attitudes are emphasized by the supporting architectural elements (*Figure 27*), which suggest precariousness, impermanence, unease; ordinarily such architecture would serve as a firm and reassuring base for the sculptured bodies, no matter what their tormented attitudes.

During the years, filled with interruptions, that he worked on the Medici tombs, Italy was invaded by Austrian and Spanish troops. In the midst of work on the tombs Michelangelo

27

Figure 28

28

became director of fortifications for Florence; he had to flee the city when it was besieged and returned after its fall in 1530. Italy's disasters and humiliations in war were bad enough; in addition, having already seen at first hand the corruption and worldliness of the Church, Michelangelo also saw the first indications of the excesses to which its Counter Reformation would go to stem the tide that threatened to engulf it.

Working against this background and harassed by personal problems, Michelangelo painted a Last Judgment (*Figure 28*) in which the blessed are all but ignored. It is a panorama of universal judgment by a Christ whose muscular exaggerations make him a terrifying and almost repellent figure. Some of the agonized sinners borne to hell turn back to regard Christ with unrepentant hatred; the wrathful Christ himself has been called Michelangelo's castigation of the times. It is usually said, also, that *The Last Judgment* suffers from exaggeration, that it loses force by the very overemphasis that makes it so terrifying. This may be true. Certainly its theme of violence limits it in comparison with the interwoven philosophical speculations offered by the Sistine Ceiling. But the moment in Rome's history and in Michelangelo's life that had inspired the timeless grandeur of the Sistine Ceiling had passed.

In the history of painting Michelangelo's revolutionary influence was the most decisive since Giotto's. From Giotto through Masaccio and the Renaissance to Raphael we can trace a steady progression based on investigating reality as a means of discovering inner harmony. Michelangelo disrupts this progression. Instead of harmony as the Renaissance had conceived it, he releases inner turbulence, departing from reality to depict often physically impossible contortions of natural forms.

Michelangelo was a hurtling force whose impact was so great that it shifted the direction painting had been following for more than two hundred years. That his immediate influence was tremendous is dramatically apparent in the paintings of the Venetian artist Jacopo Robusti, called Tintoretto (1518–1594).

Tintoretto

"*Disegno di Michelangelo e colori di Tiziano*" (the drawing of Michelangelo and the color of Titian)—Tintoretto is said to have inscribed these words over the door to his studio. If he did not, he might well have. Present-day critics would scribble beneath them, "and the individualistic esthetic cultivation of the mannerists," for Tintoretto has also been placed on the fringes of a movement that is becoming a catchall for everyone who departed from the classical ideal during the mid-century crisis.

Tintoretto, a full generation younger than Michelangelo and Titian, was in his early twenties when Michelangelo completed *The Last Judgment* (1541) and when Titian had entered his richest period. Tintoretto's *Baptism of Christ* (Plate E12) shows well enough the drawing of one and the color of the other. But it is not what he combined but what he added of his own that makes Tintoretto more than a minor artist. The bursting incandescence and the flowing, twisting forms revealed in dramatized areas of dark shade and blazing light—these are Tintoretto's own. The figure of John the Baptist, particularly, thrusts forth into light and recedes into dark or is reduced to a silhouette (as is the head) against glowing pulsations of gold and blue. Everywhere the picture is more insistent than a Titian. It demands our attention, and when our attention threatens to wander it adds a light or forces a dark or displays an exceptionally theatrical twist of the brush or turns a figure in sudden change of direction to catch our eye and, above all, to stir our emotional response.

In all these ways Tintoretto leads us out of his century—he died in its last decade—into the age of the baroque in the triumphant century that is the subject of our next portfolio.

Color Plates

Figures in the Text